P9-ASB-670

THE LITTLE HILL

Poems & Pictures by
Harry Behn

HARCOURT, BRACE & WORLD, INC.
NEW YORK

D.2.64

PRINTED IN THE UNITED STATES
OF AMERICA

TO

PAMELA

PRESCOTT

&

PETER

CONTENTS

THE LITTLE HILL

GARDENS

Clouds are flowers
Around the sun.

The summer breeze
Hums with bees.

One drop of dew
Holds only me,

But there is one
That holds the sun

And clouds and flowers
And everyone.

THE WAVE

There were lonesome birds on a misty shore,
And a kind of a far-off rumbling roar,
And creatures that dig in the sand to hide,
And empty shells at the edge of a tide.
The water was blue and smooth and wide –
It was only a tired old sea.

Then slowly a big wave grew and grew,
A white wave spilled from the top of the blue
And roared up the shore to splash me! Instead,
It splashed itself, and curled back to its bed
Like a tired old dragon not quite dead –
But dragons don't frighten me!

CAT & CACTUS

Birds, beware!
There,
That
Is a cat
Hiding claws
In velvet paws.

Rest, my sweet!
Sweet
Rest
In cactus nest —
No bird was torn
By an honest thorn.

THIS HAPPY DAY

Every morning when the sun
Comes smiling up on everyone,
It's lots of fun
To say good morning to the sun.
  Good morning, Sun!

Every evening after play
When the sunshine goes away,
It's nice to say,
Thank you for this happy day,
  This happy day!

MR. PYME

Once upon a time
Old Mr. Pyme
Lived all alone
Under a stone.

When the rain fell
He rang a bell,
When the sun shined
He laughed and dined

And floated to town
On thistle down,
And what a nice time
Had Mr. Pyme!

CIRCLES

The things to draw with compasses
Are suns and moons and circleses
And rows of humptydumpasses
Or anything in circuses
Like hippopotamusseses
And hoops and camels' humpasses
And wheels on clownses busseses
And fat old elephumpasses.

GROWING UP

When I was seven
We went for a picnic
Up to a magic
Foresty place.
I knew there were tigers
Behind every boulder,
Though I didn't meet one
Face to face.

When I was older
We went for a picnic
Up to the very same
Place as before,
And all of the trees
And the rocks were so little
They couldn't hide tigers
Or *me* any more.

THE LITTLE HILL

Windy shadows race
Over a hilly place
I know, a sunny place,
  A secret place.

It's not so far away,
I go there every day,
Every bright windy day
  I go there to play.

Over the garden wall
I climb and jump and fall
Into weeds by the wall,
  And then I crawl

As quiet as can be
Under a hollow tree
Where once a bumble bee
  Bumbled at me.

Then still, so very still
Through shade I go until
I see my little hill
  Sunny and still.

Up through the pleasant sun
Up to the top I run
Higher than everyone
  Under the sun,

High up until I see
Over the tallest tree,
Over town to the sea,
  The blue sea . . .

Here no one ever goes
Because here nothing grows,
Only weeds and wild rose,
  And no one knows

Hidden by woods and vine
Far up in the sun shine
This little hill is mine,
  This hill is mine.

SPRING

The last snow is going,
Brooks are overflowing,
A sunny wind is blowing
  Swiftly along.

Through sky birds are blowing,
On earth green is showing,
You can feel earth growing
  Quiet and strong.

A sunny wind is blowing,
Farmer's busy sowing,
Apple trees are snowing,
  And shadows grow long.

Now the wind is slowing,
Cows begin lowing,
Evening clouds are glowing
  And dusk is full of song.

FIRST DAY AT SCHOOL

At school today, my very first day,
I learned it's a place where they make you play,
Like A is for Apple and B for Bat
And C is to see some kind of a Cat.

I learned how pencils smell and the taste,
Though you mustn't eat it, of library paste,
And how to add two take-away-two,
And how to mix all the colors for blue,

And America God-bless our school,
And hippity-hop and the Golden Rule,
And how to draw with a piece of chalk
So it makes a wonderful screechy squawk!

DIFFERENT THINGS

Cows don't play hop-scotch
Any more than pigs,
Kittens never cackle ever
The way a dog digs,
The way bees buzz or birds fly
Or bubbles float or babies cry.
Still, why they do or don't it seems
I only understand in dreams.

Some times I wonder
If it wouldn't be fun
To let the trees go where they please
Or make the moon the sun.
But then my shoes would be my hat,
And so I leave things this or that
About the way they are, but funny
Like breadandbuttercups and honey.

SANDY TIN McCANN

Billy asked his father,
Father said no,
Dogs in apartments
Simply don't go.

Billy wasn't happy
But Billy wasn't sad,
He just got busy
With what he had.

He borrowed mother's scissors
And a nice tin can
And cut and cut until he'd made
Sandy Tin McCann.

Sandy was supposed to be
A little scotty pup
With two ears crinkled down
Tail crinkled up.

But when Billy finished
And sicked him on the cat,
Sandy grumbled, *Hoot Mon!*
Just like that.

The trouble was that Sandy
Had set his mind to be
Anything, but *not* a dog,
No, not he!

Billy wasn't too sad
When Sandy wouldn't play,
He bandaged up his thumb,
Put the scissors away,

And left old Sandy
In the trash can, hooting,
While he went all alone
To Scotland, scooting.

RAINDROPS

They tap like fingers on the window pane,
But they aren't fingers, they are only rain.

They fall the way bees do into a flower,
But they aren't bees, they're pieces of a shower.

They jump in puddles just like little men,
Then they aren't ever even rain again,

They're simply water wrinkled by the motion
Of streams and rivers till they're only ocean.

But oceans turn to waves, and waves to spray
And mist that shimmers on a sunny day

And floats across the sky above the shrouds
Of ships until it folds up into clouds.

Then raindrops fall again. Unless they're snow.
My teacher told me this, and so it's so.

ADVENTURE

It's not very far to the edge of town
Where trees look up and hills look down,
We go there almost every day
To climb and swing and paddle and play.

It's not very far to the edge of town,
Just up one little hill and down,
And through one gate, and over two stiles —
But coming home it's miles and miles.

NAP TIME

At nap time all my shades are drawn
Because when sunshine on our lawn
Falls much too quiet, then the bees
Buzzing around our apple trees
May not be bees at all, but Things
That hurt you worse than bites and stings,
They might be little dragons even,
Or small bad angels out of heaven.

Of course, not everything would go
Out where sunshine glistens so,
Not everything — but Things would dare!
I've seen them drifting in the air
Dancing like feathers across our lawn.
That's why my window shades are drawn!
I hear them whirr and fly and creep
And whisper — till I fall asleep.

SWING SONG

Oh I've discovered
A happy thing!
For every game
There's a song to sing,
Sometimes with words
Sometimes without,
It's easy to tell
What a song's about
From only a humming
Like wind at noon,
It needn't be even
Half a tune
If only it goes
With what you do,
If what you do
Is exactly true,
Or anyway if
It seems to you.

The time I discovered
This wonderful thing
I really was swinging
In a swing,
And the song I was singing
Was just as true
For all the flying
Sky-things too,

For seagulls and eagulls
And bees and bugs
And arrows and sparrows,
Enchanted rugs,
Clouds and balloons,
Balloons and bees —
A backward humming
A forward breeze,
Swinging without
Any tune you please.

TREES

Trees are the kindest things I know,
They do no harm, they simply grow

And spread a shade for sleepy cows,
And gather birds among their boughs.

They give us fruit in leaves above,
And wood to make our houses of,

And leaves to burn on Hallowe'en,
And in the Spring new buds of green.

They are the first when day's begun
To touch the beams of morning sun,

They are the last to hold the light
When evening changes into night,

And when a moon floats on the sky
They hum a drowsy lullaby

Of sleepy children long ago . . .
Trees are the kindest things I know.

BANTAM ROOSTER

He woke me with his tiny trill,
And snow was on the window sill.

He only hatched last Spring, but he
Is big as ever he will be.

I wish I could become a man
As quickly as a bantam can,

Why, right this morning I would go
A hundred miles across the snow!

EARLY

Before the sun was quite awake
I saw the darkness like a lake
Float away in a little stream
As swift and misty as a dream.

It left the morning oh so still
Except once a whippoorwill
Up in the orchard whispered a word
And once a frog trilled like a bird.

Then I could only think of me,
And what a nicer child I'd be
If I could learn to walk as still
As morning sunlight on a hill.

RUINS

Some very nice persons have no use for things
Of wind and rust and dust with wings,
Or dust that broods in the sun and sings,

But I like noons when it's hot and dusty,
And cellars that are damp and musty,
And windmills especially when they're rusty.

I like an orchard gone to seed
In thistles and gourd and tangles of weed,

I like a mossy trough that spills,
And old machinery left on hills,

Deserted barns and earthy smells,
And water shining in old wells.

I like the rumble of a warm
Cloud gathering a thunderstorm,

And gusts of wind that whirl and fall,
And stillness, and a dove's call.

Some very nice persons have no use for things
Of wind and rust and dust with wings,
Or dust that broods in the sun and sings,

But what may seem like ruins of a wall
For me hasn't changed very much at all
From the castle it was, and I hear the call

Of children who lived here long ago
Still beautiful and sunny and slow,
And the secret they know, I seem to know.

LISTENING

I can hear kittens and cows and dogs
And cooing pigeons and grumpy frogs
And hundreds of pleasant far-off things
Like beetles snapping shut their wings
And chuffing trains and bells and walking
And people on the corner talking,

But when my mother calls to know
Why I'm so everlasting slow,
Or will I please stay off the lawn,
Or come and put my sweater on,
Then even when I'm very near
I honestly don't seem to hear.

WAITING

Dreaming of honeycombs to share
With her small cubs, a mother bear
Sleeps in a snug and snowy lair.

Bees in their drowsy, drifted hive
Sip hoarded honey to survive
Until the flowers come alive.

Sleeping beneath the deep snow
Seeds of honeyed flowers know
When it is time to wake and grow.

UNDINE'S GARDEN

I wonder what it might be like
  Under the sea?
I know, said little Undine, sighing
  Wistfully,
I know, I know, because I live
  Under the sea.

When I look up I see no sun,
My silver sky
Shines back a topsy-turvy world
In which am I
Till swans like feathery white clouds
Go floating by,

And then the ripples weave your sun
Into my sea
In golden webs that sift and sparkle
Over me
And settle through a waving branch
Of coral tree.

My colored leaves and vines are bright
Beyond compare,
Shimmering bubbles grow like flowers
Everywhere
Drifting unopened as they float
Up to the air,

And in and out like flying birds
Little fish
Go nibbling at the swaying vines,
They dart and swish
Silent in my garden — song
Is my one wish!

HALLOWE'EN

Tonight is the night
When dead leaves fly
Like witches on switches
Across the sky,
When elf and sprite
Flit through the night
On a moony sheen.

Tonight is the night
When leaves make a sound
Like a gnome in his home
Under the ground,
When spooks and trolls
Creep out of holes
Mossy and green.

Tonight is the night
When pumpkins stare
Through sheaves and leaves
Everywhere,
When ghoul and ghost
And goblin host
Dance round their queen.
It's Hallowe'en!

COLORING

A rake, a coat, a meadow, a mill,
A cake, a boat, a house on a hill,
A kite, a spade, and a ball of string,
A wind in the leaves, and the song birds sing –
  It's Spring!
We're outdoors coloring
Every bright beautiful wonderful thing.

Under a lilac bush we've made
A studio with walls of shade,
And in our painting books we spread
Pools of yellow, blue, and red –
  Carefully,
Though it doesn't matter
Terribly much unless we spatter.

Green and red, and there's a tree
With apples and cherries, and here's a sea
With a wave and a sky and a gull in flight,
And this is the sun splashing light –
  It's Spring!
We're coloring, and all the birds sing
Of every bright beautiful wonderful thing!

THUNDERSTORM

The sun looked down at the wide wide land
That was his to shine upon, his to command,
He looked and he looked at the big blue hill
And all he wanted was to look his fill.
He just loved floating in the bright blue sky
Simply looking, but he heaved a sigh
As he watched the big blue ocean below
Weaving sparkles to and fro

Only more brightly than a weaver weaves,
And he watched the bushes building leaves,
And a little brook no wider than your hand
Running bravely through desert sand.

With everyone so busy, the sun up high
Gave a grunt and a chuckle, "Well, who am I
Not to do *my* share?" And that's when he
Filled up a pail with a sparkling sea.
Heavy as it was, he trudged up the hill
Trying his best not to splash or spill.

Not far above went a fat old cloud
With his nose in the air and very very proud
Sailing along without looking, as if
He weren't sailing smack at a steep sharp cliff!
It would have been simple to go around,
But *he* was too important! What the sun found
When he finally climbed up high enough to see
Was that fat old proud cloud snagged on a tree
On the steep sharp cliff, and was he stuck!
Wheezing and bulging and cursing his luck.

The sun sat down on the hill near by
And watched for a while with a smile in his eye.

"It seems you're stuck," he said, "pretty bad."
But the way he said it made the cloud mad.
"I am," puffed the cloud, "and it's thanks to you
For leaving this big blue hill in the view!"
He tried to be proud but it wasn't much use,
He was tired out trying to pry himself loose.

The sun yawned politely. He was tired, too.
He sneezed and said, "I'll tell you what to do,
Tighten up your lightning bolts, give a nudge!"
The cloud gave a heave, and still didn't budge.
The sun sort of chuckled to himself, and there
Sat the two of them glaring, glare for glare.

Along came the wind who was shaking out seeds
From pods of bushes and flowers and weeds.
He saw the sun so he rushed and he twirled
Puffing out seeds all over the world,
Puffing until he was tired to death
So *he* sat down to catch *his* breath.
You know how the wind is, couldn't keep still,
He talked about business the way people will.
"Take dandelions, for instance, what do they care
They have their silly children everywhere,
But when do they ever do a single thing

About them, summer or winter or spring!
They keep on having them even in the fall,
And *I* am the one has to sow them all."

The sun and the cloud both looked away,
So the wind didn't have much else to say
Except, "Very well, then!" He rubbed his cheek
And waited for somebody else to speak.
When nobody did, he went back to work
And shook a big oak tree, gave it such a jerk
He yanked it out of the hill with a crash,
And down came the tree with a smash and a flash
And a boom and a rumble so sudden and loud
It drew, very naturally, quite a crowd.

The crowd was all clouds, they came on the run,
They trampled the wind, they rumpled the sun,
And as clouds do when there's anything exciting
They bumped each other and started fighting,
They used loud language, like *thunder* and *hail*,
And thumped each other with the sun's full pail,
The pail he had lugged up with might and main,
And down came millions of gallons of rain.

The sun tried his best to be dignified
But the clouds got madder the more he tried,

They tumbled hail over thunderhead
Not listening to anything anybody said,
Till the crazy wind grabbed the proud cloud still
Snagged on the cliff of the big blue hill
And tossed him thud on a tangled heap
Of clouds by now piled eighteen deep,
Then he jumped in the middle!

The last anyone
Could see in the mess was the poor old sun
Worried but smiling, or *trying* to smile,
Way, way down on the bottom of the pile.
And all he had wanted with a kindly sigh
Was simply to float in a bright blue sky.

THANK YOU

Dear Santa Claus, Dear Aunty Sue,
Dear Uncle George and Grandma, you
Were very kind to send me such
Nice presents, thank you very much.
How did you know I wanted sox
And hankies in a pretty box,
And wool pajamas and a pair
Of slippers and new underwear?
Thank you very much for knowing
Just my size, the way I'm growing.
I liked them very much, and thank
You for the lovely savings bank.
Also the scrubbing brush and soap
Were very nice, too, and I hope
You had a happy Christmas day.
My toys are swell! Now may I play?

THE MERRY-GO-ON

With a huff and a puff
And a chuff-chuff-chuff
The merry-go-round began,
And little white Horse
Heaved off on a course
Around to the ticket man.

The music played
And Tiger swayed
Too dreamy even to roar,
Not seeming to turn he
Went on on his journey
To just where he was before.

Lion pounced
And Zebra bounced,
But all of the beasts were tame
In the middle of Spring
Where every thing
Goes round and around the same.

Except for Swan
Who was fastened on
Floating around in one place,
The animals seemed
Like creatures dreamed
In a happy-go-round kind of race

Where Elephant led,
Gazelle was ahead,
And first was Kangaroo,
And tall Giraffe
Laughed a long laugh
Because he was winning, too.

Only one beast
Was just the least
Uncertain about the race —
He seemed to find
They were *all* behind
And his was the very last place!

Not to be first
Was about the worst
Place that ever could be,
And so as soon
As the tinkly tune
Stopped for a change, then he

Decided that when
It started again
He'd make very sure *he* led —
He'd stop going round
And see what he found
By going straight on instead!

This creature, of course,
Was little white Horse
Who did what he planned to do,
He went straight on
Across the wide lawn
Into the forest and through.

Happy and free
As a horse can be,
On and on he ran —
And that was the way
One April day
The merry-go-on began.

Happy and free
As a horse can be
Was Horse with no one ahead,
Till he looked behind
Only to find
Nobody there to be led.

It was true as true
The world was a new
And strange and beautiful place,
But a race is no fun
Already won
Because there is no one to race.

So Horse stood still
On a lonesome hill
And looked at a lonesome view
Beyond the sound
Of the merry-go-round,
And he wondered what to do.

At last he knew
Why so very few
Or rather he knew why none
Of his friends had ever
Never, never
Done what he had done.

So far away
Was the happy play
Of galloping to a song,
The golden ring,
And the ding-ding-ding
Of the starting and stopping gong.

But here was only
A very lonely
Place that was awfully still.
Well, that was that
And so he sat
Waiting, waiting — until

A little Child
Came up and smiled
And asked if Horse was lost,
And if he was
Then how much does
A merry-go-on ride cost?

Horse said that he
Was sure it was free,
And so the child climbed on.
Away they flew
From the lonesome view
Back to the woods and the lawn.

Back to his place
In the happy-go-race
Went Horse, and no one found
That Child and he
Had been free as free,
And he galloped round and around.

But children know
When off they go
On the back of that one white Horse
The tinkly tune
Will change soon,
And so will they, of course,

From around and about
To away, way out
To a place where it's always dawn,
Where children see
What always will be
On the merry-go-on-and-on.

SPRING RAIN

Leaves make a slow
Whispering sound
As down the drops go
Drip to the ground.
  Peace, peace, says the tree.

Good wet rain!
Shout happy frogs,
Peepers and big green
Bulls in bogs,
  Lucky, lucky are we!

On a bough above,
Head under wing,
A mourning dove
Waits time to sing.
  Ah me, she sighs, ah me!

ALMOST

Peterboo and Prescott
And pretty Pam, too,
Are very many children
But they know what to do,

They eat all their cereal
And crusts of their bread,
They never need spankings,
They go quietly to bed,

They hang up their clothes,
They practice when they should,
And their manners are always
Exceptionally good.

This little poem
Is about Peterboo
And Pamela and Prescott —
And it's *almost* true.